Drivers' Ed for the Brain

"I am a counselor at a substance abuse disorder clinic and have been using *Drivers' Ed for the Brain* with my patients. The format is easy for my patients to relate to and it helps improve their lives. They are better able to navigate the difficult emotional path that many who suffer from addiction face in recovery, when they apply these simple tools. I would recommend this book to anyone looking for a fresh new way to navigate the road of life."

—Dianna Murphy, LCSW

"*Drivers' Ed for the Brain* is a great and good reminder about the true importance of the here and now and not to look for compensatory patterns by deviating, consciously or not, towards past or future events. The lessons contained in the book are important to help promote courageous and conscious acts that allow us to finally know who we are, where we are, and how we act in the face of life's challenges.

"The book is an excellent practical contribution, to obtain healthier, more present and conscious thought patterns. The book provides good advice to discover, understand, and modify those unconscious patterns that we inherit and/or acquire throughout our life experience. The great contribution that Mr. Ryan J. Hulbert gives us in his book is to connect in a single state (present), the transcendent of the everyday simple circumstances of our life, and our active and meaningful relationship with the decisions of each of them."

—Carlos Pezoa Correa,
Professional Technical Establishment Instructor

"I enjoyed this concise and clear, but simple read about how we choose to use our minds in our lives. Dr. Hulbert gives a clear case of understanding to show us the difference between dwelling in the past, fearing the future, and living in the present. The metaphor of driving a car and the lessons displayed fit very well for virtually everyone in our modern society about how we can focus our attention in creating a joyful and peaceful life. I would recommend this book to anyone interested in understanding themselves and how we have the power to manifest our own lives."

—Joe Thames Gundy,
Author and Professor of Conflict Management

"I would like to thank Dr. Ryan Hulbert for his excellent and effective work. I was proud of my contribution to work with him and learned from him many ideas and ways to lead the mind and think positively. We were all an integrated Arab team of the lessons for *Drivers' Ed for the Brain*. We functioned with the ideas of the lessons so we loved working together and we wanted to learn from the bottom of our hearts. About me personally, my presence in this experience was regarded as a gift from God and it was a worthy opportunity. I hope everyone who does the lessons has many answers to many questions."

—Sura llyas,
Arabic Translator for an Iraqi women's group

"I really enjoyed the book. As a reader I like that the book was short so it seemed doable to finish it even if you don't have much time, which seemed important in my busy schedule. I think the book is well linked to local realities of life. Coming to the U.S. I understood that driving is a big part of life, and as I had to learn to drive recently myself, the analogy with the car and driving laid so easy on my fresh knowledge. I found it to be the best explanation of the benefits of being in the present I have met so far. As I am a counselor, I recently was looking for examples to bring up to my client how the connection of the body, mind and spirit can help him in solving psychological problems. In the book I discovered a very good resource of simple but powerful explanations that I can use. My most favorite way to shift gears is to connect to nature. I used to think that when I immerse myself in nature, look at green grass, trees, and fields, I can return to myself and feel inspiration. But since I moved to the States it seemed that it stopped working for me because the sceneries here are different. I couldn't find quite the same picture anywhere around. Reading the book I tried the exercises and understood that the most important sense for me was actually smell. I started dedicating more time appreciating smells. And bingo! It worked."

—Irina Chernyshkova,
Couselor and Russian Translator

"There are books that are a true labyrinth for the common reader, that reader who seeks to enjoy reading, and to make this process his partner in time and the light that illuminates his mind. *Drivers' Ed for the Brain*, with a title that could seem almost labyrinthine, the book gathers, nevertheless, for the less educated reader and also for the others, those requirements that make reading an enjoyment that benefits the body, feeds the mind and transports the spirit to an immeasurable world 'of greater peace and joy.' This book shows that its author moves naturally from 'the simple to the complex' and from 'the concrete to the abstract' and that his methodology, to make the topics of psychological depth understood, does not displace the less erudite reader, but entails a deep knowledge of the art of teaching. I remember here the words of someone who said: 'If the good is short, it is twice as good,' which fits perfectly for this book that gives a clear and profound message of how to find the seemingly lost path to a more pleasant life."

— Luis Guerra Jaque,
Retired School Teacher

"In Drivers' Ed for the Brain are little lessons filled with great wisdom and clear, concise instructions on how to live a better, more fulfilling life. In simple, easy to understand language, it guides the participant to learn how to meet the challenges of everyday life from a more spiritually alert and sensory filled perspective. I feel privileged to have the opportunity to work on the translation of such valuable materials, hoping that my work can eventually help Spanish people everywhere have access to this important knowledge, so they too can feel inspired to change the narratives of their own lives, and improve the quality of their lives' journey."

— **Claudia Guerra Labarca,**
Translator of the book in Spanish

"I loved your book *Drivers' Ed for the Brain*. It really helped me open up my mind and calm down and think about when like I get upset or angry to calm down. Like the shifting gear part. Like when you dwell on your anger you're like sitting in 1st gear. And I've noticed I do that a lot. So when I'm free I definitely am going to work on shifting by using my mind and body. Also, I would love a copy of the book! It's very useful. Maybe write another. But make it longer."

— **17-year-old girl,**
from a juvenile deterntion facility

"I have personally used the roadmap to realize that I was not on the road and used the gears to center myself."

— **17-year-old boy,**
from a juvenile detention facility

"Before I read the book, I was considering therapy because I've had a lot of issues with emotional management. This book helped a lot with that, and I printed out the diagrams to help me with tracking my emotions. I don't feel like I need therapy as much as I did before. I felt like there was something wrong with me because I couldn't identify what was going on in my head because it always looked so easy for everyone else and I couldn't put a name on my emotions. But now I don't think I need therapy. I'm able to put a label on what I'm feeling and track how I'm feeling by realizing what gear I'm in and to take a moment and smarten myself up again."

— Lillie Scofield,
Sophmore at a Medical Arts Charter High School

"I felt like this book has some really practical advice in it. Most importantly, I like the analogy of the airplane and having perspective on our problems. Along with this, the importance of recognizing a positive mood and its influence on perspective comes into play. I can see times in my past where I have been overwhelmed with a situation and recognize that my mood was low or negative. I see other times where in the same situation and my mood was on a higher plane that I am able to make better judgments. Another important insight I learned was trying to live in the present. Right now I am probably at one of the busiest times in my life and I am constantly thinking about the tasks that need to be completed. I recognize that I need to slow down and pay attention to people when they are speaking to me (I pride myself on being a dual-task expert, but I'm realizing that should not be the most important priority). I am focusing on trying to have a balance between mostly living in the present but learning from the past and setting goals for the future."

— Dixie Seegmiller,
mother and grandmother

"When I started reading this book I was confused, stressed, and afraid of going back to that feeling of darkness called depression. The title of the book immediately struck me as interesting. As I read it, I began to understand what was happening to me, and how I could solve it. I found that, in a simple way, this wonderful book guides us and helps us to get rid of all those things that make our life more complex; things that we accumulate inside that we can change, in order to enjoy what we have in the present and achieve the goal for which we are living here."

— Lissette Vallejos, mother

"This book was very helpful. I think that most people probably don't know what a healthy state of mind looks like. If someone has been anxious or worrisome for most of their life, they may think that this is normal, and that everyone feels this way. The material in this book explains both what a healthy mind looks like, and provides the tools for any willing individual to achieve such a state of mind. My favorite part of the book was the lesson about the road, and how we need to be in the present and not stray too far off to the past or the future. This really resonates with me because even though the past and future are both important, the present is where we really need to be, or we will miss our whole lives. I also like the analogy of the airplane, because it shows that there is a right and wrong way to look at the past and the future."

— **Bynrose Foote,**
Female College Student

"I have struggled with PTSD, formally diagnosed for some time now. I've been to nine different therapists, two psychiatrists, tried EMDR therapy, and have even been admitted to a mental health facility for a brief time. I have tried numerous different types of therapy in many different places, and with people from many different walks of life, and I have yet to find a more interactive, beneficial, and accommodating tool than *Drivers' Ed for the Brain*. With life becoming increasingly busy, it has become difficult to maintain a constant schedule with any one therapist. This book has allowed me to continue my therapy from a metacognitive standpoint. The exercises help me reconnect and get back to the present; something that has been previously very difficult for me. Sometimes I feel like I am a balloon and am floating while watching life go by. This tool helps me stay grounded. In times when I begin to overthink, dwell, or panic, the breathing exercises have been wonderful. My boyfriend of two years didn't know or understand anything about mental health before meeting me. He tries really hard to understand where I am coming from. When I start to panic he now has tools to try and help me too. *Drivers' Ed for the Brain* has not only helped me, but also my relationships and perspectives of the world around me."

— **Female College Student**

"After reading *Drivers' Ed for the Brain* I came out feeling like a much more positive person with a very positive and confident outlook on my current life. I say "current" because one of the biggest concepts I took away from this book is to focus on the here and now. Live in the present and appreciate what life is and what it has to offer. Make connections with people and find joy through helping other people find joy. I really enjoyed this book and how it was based around the story, but it was able to intertwine the important concepts and ideas of living a self-fulfilling life in a very interesting attention-grabbing way. I would recommend this book to just about anybody because it can really help one to look past the base layer of stress, anger, and other negative thoughts we find ourselves buried in, and see that life is full of many more important things that are much more worthy of our mental time and energy. It's actually easier to be happy than it is to be negative!"

— **Nick Parisi,**
Male College Student

"The book *Drivers' Ed for the Brain* written by Ryan J Hulbert, slowly involves readers in reflections on very deep and often times unconscious aspects of our life, and its sometimes meaningless dynamics, automated habits, thoughts, actions. These are those games that our mind plays and prevents us from living here and now, enjoy the moment, treasure what we have without spending emotional energy to solve the problems that have not happened yet, constant effort to change something that is long gone in the past. This is the fight with 'wind mills' that exhaust us, without yielding any result. We are held hostage in our past and future, forgetting that we live in the present. We are so focused on our everyday routine that oftentimes we do not notice many beautiful things that we encounter every day, such as the smell of hot chocolate, child's laughter, or a playful kitten. Stories, examples and emotions, or people from the book from the very beginning start influencing your own life, how you perceive it and makes you reevaluate your old directives. The book is based on examples of other peoples' feelings and impressions that every one of us can easily understand. Because of that it seems that every page asks you a question, the answer to which you already know in your head. And that knowledge makes you feel that all the answers are inside of us, that we are the biggest source of energy, strength and knowledge to be able to manage our lives. This book is like a manual, a hint on what to do, those 'old good friends' that will give you the words you need when you need to hear them. Dr. Vreda is in a sense our internal voice that makes us stop in this sometimes crazy world and feel yourself, hear your body, your consciousness, and through these feelings become turned on in your life and start feeling its taste."

—Nadya Potter-Lupashko

"Before I read *Drivers' Ed for the Brain*, I thought theories on psychology were deep, abstract and metaphysical. Those psychological ideas and techniques for me look reasonable but lack of methodological significance. Dr. Hulbert's book totally changes my impression on psychology. Adopting novel approach and using many practical examples which everybody could face in his/her life, the author makes psychological theories easy to understand and the techniques, like taking deep breath, doing the activities involving both mind and body and so forth, are easy to put into practice.

"With the pace of modern life getting faster and faster, people nowadays face the heavy pressure of all kinds. It is easy for us to become unhealthy or subhealthy psychologically and keep staying in such state for long unconsciously. Dr. Hulbert's book points out clearly the features of such unhealthy or sub-healthy state (first gear) which will make it easy for people to recognize themselves in the first gear and to use techniques to change in time. This year the daughter of one of my friends will graduate from primary school. She wants to choose a good middle school for her daughter but it is really not easy in China. Her daughter's education problem keeps pressing on her. One day, influenced by my friend's anxiety, I began to feel anxious about my daughter's education, too. I pictured that I would face the same problem as my friend when my daughter graduated from primary school. The more I thought, the more anxious I felt, as if my daughter had already gone to a bad middle school. At this moment, Dr. Hulbert's psychological ideas crossed my mind. I suddenly realized that my daughter was only a seven-year-old primary school student right now. I was worried about the things that would happen far into the future. I was totally out of present at that time. How ridiculous I was! I told myself to stop thinking and get a sound sleep. 'Tomorrow is another day.' On the second day, I felt much better. My mind was clearer. I thought that I still had five years and believed that I could make a good plan for my daughter in such a long time.

"Dr. Hulbert's *Drivers' Ed for the Brain* works for me and I believe it will also work for you! Please give it a try!"

—**Amy Sun**

"Being a native German, I enjoyed reading this book, *Drivers'
Ed for the Brain* in my native tongue. I regret that I did not
have this opportunity in my younger years, as it would have
been very helpful raising children and coping with the change
of culture. Now as I have advanced in years, the Drivers'
Training… analogy makes the information more understand-
able. I am practicing many of Dr. Hulbert's principles and feel
increasing success and happiness. It is a book that I would like
to share with others, young and old."

—Beate Hofmann Cook

Drivers' Ed
for the Brain

"FINDING GREATER PEACE & JOY"

Drivers' Ed
for the Brain

"FINDING GREATER PEACE & JOY"

Ryan J. Hulbert, Ph.D.

Revised design by Elena Van Horn.

ISBN — 13: 979-8441722506

Independently Published

First Edition: 2015

Printed in the U.S.

To my mother, Olive: one of the best drivers I know.

—RJH

Foreword

"The idea of Drivers' Ed for the Brain delights me to no end. A novel approach to engaging the interest, particularly of our young, in how they might get better control of their own behavior and have some idea of its fundamentals.

For many people, driving a vehicle is a source of greater freedom and opportunity. Dr. Hulbert's book is like an engaging manual for experiencing that greater freedom to find increased peace and joy in our lives.

Through stories, enlightening metaphors, and practical examples, this book serves as a personal driving coach for both safety and soaring on our journey of life. I highly recommend it to all, young and old alike."

—**Dr. Virgil A. Wood**, ten year working associate of Dr. Martin Luther King, Jr., and author of *In Love We Trust: Lessons I learned from Martin Luther King, Jr. and Sr.*

Contents

Introduction

A new beginning—that's what Rob and Linda were looking for when they decided to pull up roots and move to their new state. There had been several years of gradually increasing stress as their four children, ranging in ages from fourteen to seven, were growing up.

Rob and Linda seemed to be growing apart, and Rob's career dreams had not panned out. They agreed to stay with Linda's parents, hopefully for only a month or two, to figure out where to go from there.

Rob had asked his wife for directions to the County Court House to get a drivers' license for his new state. It was a sunny but somewhat chilly spring morning. The trees were covered with new buds. "A good time to make a new start," he thought to himself as he attempted to gather some hope and determination as he drove to the courthouse.

At the courthouse, Rob recalled how he felt when going for his first drivers' license test as a teenager. He remembered the challenges of drivers' education, nervously taking the written driving test, being informed that he had passed, and seeing the big smile on his photo ID.

As he walked by a bulletin board near the entrance to the Drivers' License Bureau, his eye caught sight of an advertisement for drivers' ed. He paused to read the announcement, which stated:

DRIVERS' ED FOR THE BRAIN

Come and enjoy a community education class at the public library Tuesday nights from 7:00–8:00 pm for six weeks

Learning Objectives:

- Using your mind, body, and spirit for a less stressed filled ride.
- Using the proper mental gears to meet your challenges.
- Understanding the road conditions on your life journey.
- Using the right fuel to have more inspiration in meeting your challenges.
- Piloting on a spiritual plane.
- Following the map to a more joyful life!

Costs: Just for materials

Hope to see you there!

The class seemed interesting to him and he thought about it on the way home. As Rob returned to his in-laws' home with new license in hand, he told his wife about the bulletin he had seen and his hope to attend the class. Linda told him that it sounded interesting, but she probably wouldn't go because of the need to be home with the children. Maybe he could pass along any ideas he found helpful.

Chapter One

A CENTURY OF DRIVING

Five days later, Rob arrived at the public library about twenty minutes early, relieved that he had been able to find it so easily. A librarian gave him directions to the conference room where the class was being held and enthusiastically whispered, "You're going to love the class! I took it last year."

At this point he had no idea who the instructor was and was even more curious about the whole class. As he entered the conference room, he saw a man he guessed to be about 60 years old, standing at the end of a table looking over some papers. Rob asked if this was Drivers' Ed for the Brain. The instructor smiled and said, "Yes, it is. Welcome!"

Rob was later to learn that Dr. Vreda was a retired psychologist who liked to stay involved in teaching and community service, through this class as well as periodically writing a column for the local newspaper. A few more class participants arrived, with each of them being greeted in a friendly manner by Dr. Vreda. A couple of them laughed as they greeted him and joked about needing a tune-up and wanting to take the class again. Dr. Vreda joked back that one of the reasons he enjoyed teaching the class was to remind himself of the main points of the lessons. A quick count by Rob showed thirteen students, including himself.

Dr. Vreda gave a brief overview of the class and encouraged class participation with comments or questions. He said that he had gleaned the materials from a variety of sources through the years, that the points had been very helpful for him personally, and that he was excited to share the ideas with the class. He encouraged them to share any points that they personally found helpful. Then he jumped in with the night's topic, which he called "A Century of Driving".

"We are going to begin with a brief history of driving, and let's focus on the last one hundred years. What were most people driving a hundred years ago? A woman raised her hand and said, "I guess a horse and buggy?"

"That's right! And what are the three parts of a horse and buggy to make it go?" A man answered, "The buggy, the horse, and the rider."

"Great! You're really a sharp class. We're off to a good start here! A hundred years later the vehicles we drive have three comparable parts to those of a hundred years ago. We have the body of the car, which is like the buggy, of course the driver, and now we have the engine instead of the horse. In fact, we even refer to the power of the motor as horsepower. Does anybody know what some common horsepowers are for a typical vehicle these days?" There was a brief discussion about this and a man in the class said that current engines range from about 100 to 300 horsepower.

Dr. Vreda continued, "Using the comparison of a modern vehicle to a horse and buggy, which of the three parts is most dominant? We can see that it is the engine or the horsepower. Now I would like to compare those three parts of the horse and buggy to three components of our being, namely our body, mind and spirit. We are going to let the carriage represent the body, the part of us that carries us from place to place. We are going to let the horse represent the mind or a source of power. And finally, we are going to let the person driving the buggy represent the spirit or our source of direction."

Dr. Vreda paused and said, "I realize that the comparison is not perfect, but be patient with me and I hope that it will be a useful one. The main point I would like to make from the comparison is the fact that just as over the last one hundred years the horsepower has increased dramatically in our vehicles, the tendency to rely heavily on our minds has also dramatically increased. With the explosion of information and technology, our reliance on our bodies for our day-to-day work or other activities has decreased for most people, and we have come to rely more heavily on our minds and thinking in most occupations. I would like to suggest to you that we modern people think too much. It is this overuse of our minds which contributes to being out of balance with our body and spirit. This is part of the reason we have so many difficulties with stress and inner unrest, because of having less of a balance among the three parts of our being."

Dr. Vreda sought feedback from the class members. He asked them to think of their grandfathers' professions. Several volunteered answers and mentioned the professions of teaching, truck driving, farming and factory work. Dr. Vreda pointed out how the majority of those occupations were predominantly physical, which was obvious to the class members. Dr. Vreda then asked the class members to compare those occupations to typical ones represented by those in the class or their close friends.

The obvious mental nature of the jobs was shown by their responses, which included such occupations as real estate agent, computer technician, telephone company secretary, and security officer.

Dr. Vreda continued, "The main point of this first lesson in Drivers' Ed for the Brain is that each of us in this modern age needs to slow down mentally. Ghandi is credited with saying, 'There is more to life than increasing its speed.' A slowing down of our mental activity involves allowing our minds to be more quiet on a regular basis."

A man in the class asked a question, which was very much on Rob's mind. He asked, "Are you encouraging us to not have anything on our minds?"

Dr. Vreda responded, "That's a very good question. What I am asking you to do is to trust the process of allowing the thoughts of your own mind to drift away more often. This usually occurs when we are having a greater balance in physical activity in comparison to mostly mental activity, and allows more frequent peaceful experiences, which uplift our spirits. Maybe an example will better explain this. A number of years ago, while my family and I were waiting to find our current home, we all crowded into an apartment for four months. It is a long- standing joke in my family that whenever dad makes breakfast, he always makes his favorite breakfast food-- oatmeal. One morning while in the small kitchen of that apartment, I had turned on a cassette tape to listen to some peaceful music while preparing to make my favorite breakfast. After putting the salt and oatmeal into the boiling water, I became distracted for a few moments. Suddenly, I heard the sound of oatmeal boiling over onto the stove".

"I quickly moved the pot to another burner and then switched on the overhead exhaust fan to clear away the smoke from the oatmeal on the burner. While the fan continued whirling, I turned on the sink faucet to moisten a cloth to clean up my mess. Then, as I turned off the faucet, I thought that I faintly heard something. The overhead fan continued to run until the smoke had cleared. Finally I switched off the fan, and as its motor gradually quieted, the peaceful music of the tape player emerged. It struck me that the music had been playing the whole time, but with the noise from both the fan and running water, I had not heard the music. I had, in fact, forgotten that it was playing. That music only became recognizable when the noises of the running water and fan had been eliminated. The music is like beautiful and peaceful parts of our lives which are being drowned out by the mental noise in our minds and the physical noise in our surroundings."

The same man again asked a question that Rob was asking himself, but was hesitant to say out loud. The man said, "I'm sorry, but I'm still not following you exactly.

Can you give me an example of how this could help me do something practical to improve my life?"

Dr. Vreda smiled and said, "You're really asking super questions and helping me to explain these points. Let me tell you another story that may help. One summer, while I was a college student, I had the job of painting a large older home. Day after day, while brushing on the paint, I thought about everything that I normally think about and finally ran out of things! As my thoughts drifted away one particular day, I realized that it had been ninety eight years since my mother's father was born. I had no memory of that grandfather because he had died when I was four years old. As I pondered this, I realized that each of his eight children were still living, although a couple of them were quite elderly. My brush strokes became a little more vigorous as I excitedly thought about the possibility of asking my mother and each of my aunts and uncles to write some of their memories of their father to have ready by the 100th anniversary of his birth in two years. I shared the idea with my wife, and eventually a small book was put together. Reading the book was a very uplifting experience for me and for a number of my relatives as well. A few years after the 100th anniversary of my grandfather's birth, my aunts and uncles passed away, leaving only my mother, who was the youngest child."

"To put this principle in a nut shell, as we slow down our minds and get a better balance between our mind, body, and spirit, we can better get in touch with ideas, insights, or messages that guide and uplift us. I am asking you to trust me on this one,"Dr. Vreda said with a smile.

"Your mission this week is to begin to practice increasing the balance between the use of your mind, the care of your body, and the nourishment of your spirit. Also consider sharing what we have talked about with another person. This will help you to better understand the main principles. Here's a homework sheet that may be of help to you in fulfilling the assignments."

When Rob arrived home that evening, his wife asked him what the class was like. Rob answered, "The teacher seems like a pretty nice guy. I'm not too sure about the class so far."

"What did you talk about?" asked Linda.

"Well, basically he said that modern people think too much. He compared the overuse of our thinking to the fact that car engines have grown tremendously in power over the last hundred years. He says that we're missing a lot of peace of mind and other good things by having our minds going too much and way too fast. I liked the story he told about forgetting that there was peaceful music when he had burned his breakfast," Rob said with a smile. "He even gave us some homework to do before the next class.

Hey, I guess I just did one of the assignments by telling you something I liked about the class!"

"Do you think you'll go back?" asked Linda.

"I guess so," said Rob. "I already bought the materials and it is kind of interesting."

During the course of the week, Rob was surprised to notice how busy his mind was most of the time. He became especially aware that when his children were talking to him, he frequently had to bring his mind back to what they were saying because of him having other things on his mind.

Lesson One Homework

For maximum benefit do this assignment before going to chapter two.

1. Recognize at least one time this week that you were relying too much on your mind and felt stressed and out of balance. Describe the situation briefly.

_____

_____

_____

_____

_____

_____

2. Choose at least one activity to begin practicing better care and involvement of your body on a regular basis. Do that activity at least once this week and briefly describe your experience.

_____

_____

_____

_____

_____

_____

3.Share at least one point from the lesson that you found interesting with another person. Briefly describe the experience.

_____

_____

_____

_____

_____

_____

_____

If interested, please watch the video "High Pressure Thoughts" by scanning the QR code.

Chapter Two

THE GEARS

"Welcome to lesson two," Dr. Vreda said with a smile. "Before we jump into tonight's lesson, I would like to invite you to share any comments about your experiences this week with your homework assignments."

Several people described experiences similar to Rob's, of being aware that they often had several things on their minds, and that they normally didn't even realize how much they were thinking. A couple of class members mentioned how they were feeling a little less stressed by doing a few more physical activities to relieve their stress and balance themselves a little more. One person had made a special effort to listen to some uplifting music, and give herself a break after a difficult day. After hearing the comments, Dr. Vreda said, "Those are very good observations, and I can tell that many of you have put some effort into fulfilling your assignments. I hope that you continue to be aware of those suggestions as we build on further assignments and principles for you to try."

"Okay, let's begin our lesson for tonight, which is called 'The Gears'. How many of you have driven a stick shift vehicle?" Dr. Vreda asked the class. Rob's hand went up in response, along with almost all of the other class member's hands. Dr. Vreda continued, "Have you ever had a vehicle in first gear while trying to drive too fast for first gear?" Many class members nodded, and he said, "What does the motor sound like when you are going too fast in first gear?"

Several class members, at the same time said things such as, "It's all revved up."

"That's right. People experience something very similar if we are in a certain mental state of mind, which we will call first gear. First gear is when only the mind is involved and we are dwelling on something unpleasant. As we proceed in that gear, the unpleasantness usually increases in intensity and we feel our emotional state revving up."

At that point Dr. Vreda asked for an example of a time a class member felt stuck in first gear. Rob thought for a moment, raised his hand and said, "I had a time this week when I was really concerned about being out of work. My father-in-law asked me what I wanted to do for a job. I took it that he was being critical, even though now, I don't think he was. I couldn't get it off my mind for the rest of the evening and I had a hard time going to sleep thinking about his criticism and what I was going to do for a job."

"That's a good example. Did you also have the experience of increasing intensity as your mind revved up?" asked Dr. Vreda.

Rob responded, "I hadn't thought of it at the time, but I remember feeling really frustrated when I was trying to sleep and my mind seemed to be going faster and faster."

Dr. Vreda then continued with the discussion: "If first gear is using only one aspect of our being, the mind, to grind away unproductively on something, then second gear involves using two aspects of our being, the mind and the body. This could be anything from peeling a potato to playing the piano, but involves doing a pleasant and/or productive activity that engages both the mind and the body at the same time. Can any of you give me an example of something you do that you enjoy which involves both the mind and body?" One woman mentioned how she likes to do crafts and a man said that he likes to play a guitar.

"Those are good examples. Is it clear how those activities require both the mind and the body to be engaged?" asked Dr. Vreda. Most of the class nodded in agreement.

"If first gear involves grinding away only on the mind, and second gear involves combining a productive use of both the body and the mind, then third gear consists of using the mind, body and spirit.

What I mean by involving the spirit is to do something of service for someone else--to get out of our own concerns and show concern for another person. Can anyone give me an example of third gear?" asked Dr. Vreda.

A woman raised her hand and said, "Maybe that explains it. I've often thought it was curious that when I am down in the dumps, I start making cookies and I always end up giving them away. I thought it was just a quirky thing about me."

"That is a perfect example! It also shows how deep inside we already know these things and discover them in the course of living. I want to highlight that seemingly very subtle emphasis on our intentions, attitudes, and purposes for doing service can result in a very different and more enhanced experience. You can try an experiment of doing something for another person either begrudgingly or with a sense of gratitude and purpose, and see whether the experience is a draining or an invigorating one."

"Well what about a fourth gear?" asked Dr. Vreda. "In physics, time is considered the fourth dimension, and we're going to view time as the fourth gear. To really shift into fourth gear, you do something that involves your mind, body, spirit, and something that has a sense of timelessness or permanence. For example, teaching a child to develop a skill, such as reading, can be very satisfying, in part because the child is learning a skill that will help him or her for the rest of his or her life. In contrast, buying a child an ice cream cone, if done in a healthy attitude, would probably mostly be a third gear experience, even though the experience could be part of a long-term relationship."

"What about kicking back and being in neutral?" a class member jokingly asked.

"A very good question," replied Dr. Vreda. "Can you give me an example of being in neutral?"

The same class member thought for a moment and then said, "How about watching a sunset or taking a bubble bath?"

"I would agree with you," said Dr. Vreda.

"Let's examine for a moment some of the characteristics of how the mind is operating when it is in neutral. In first gear the mind is very busy, pressured, and noisy. In neutral, however, the mind is quiet, clear, and at peace. It is allowing more pure and fresh perceptions to flow through it as opposed to rehashing old information. The comparison might be made to drinking a cool, pure glass of water, in contrast to chewing on a tough piece of meat. One refreshes while the other wears you out."

"You are already showing the first step in being able to shift gears, and that is being aware of what gear you are in," responded Dr. Vreda. "Let's look at some techniques about shifting that may be of help. I, personally, like you, have difficulty shifting out of first gear. In fact, many people are in first gear most of the time. Because of that, even though it is uncomfortable, they become so familiar with it that it almost becomes their preferred gear. It is as if they have forgotten that they have other gears, or maybe they slip into first gear so easily that it becomes natural to be there. Also, the intensity of first gear can trick you into thinking that you are really being productive. We have to practice at being aware of and realizing that the uncomfortable intensity associated with first gear is a signal that we need to shift."

"I have found that neutral is best found by not going directly from first, but by going from first gear to second gear, and then going into neutral. As an example of that,

14

remember my story of painting the house when I was in college? I was mostly using my body, and a little of my mind, and then my being shifted into neutral by itself. While in neutral, the inspiration came to record memories of my grandfather, which led me toward third gear--to be of service to others. Now that we're talking about it, I think that I actually went into fourth gear because of the timeless nature of family relationships and passing on those written memories to future generations."

"Before we wrap it up this evening, let's have a brief review and quiz," said Dr. Vreda. "What one part of your being are you using when you are in first gear?"

"The mind," most of the class members said almost in unison.

"Good," said Dr. Vreda. "What two parts of your being are you using when you are in second gear?"

"The body and the mind," a number of class members answered quickly.

"Okay, here's a little tougher question. If time is the fourth dimension, what needs to be part of an experience when you go in to fourth gear?"

People in the class were a little less quick to answer, but a man said, "When you are doing something of service to others that also lasts or continues on somehow."

"Good answer," said Dr. Vreda. "It looks like you guys have this down pretty well. Thanks for your comments and participation this evening. Are you brave souls ready for your next assignment? Here it is," said Dr. Vreda, as he passed out a sheet of paper to each class member.

On his way home, Rob was excited to tell Linda what he had learned tonight. It seemed to make sense and was both simple and profound to him. "Hey, that's kind of neat!" Linda said after Rob briefly described the four gears and then as an afterthought, he also described neutral.

"I always thought neutral was being lazy," Rob commented. "I guess it is a legitimate state of mind, but I suspect that it is going to be a hard one to find or to stay in for very long."

One evening that week, Rob was feeling frustrated after another day of working on his job resumé and making more telephone calls about job possibilities. He hadn't noticed initially that his eyes were beginning to squint and his mind narrowed into focusing on the several weeks that he and his family had been living in his in-laws' home, while he was still without work. Only after his mind started to race did he recognize that he was in first gear. He reflected on it for a moment, went back into first gear, and smiled slightly as he realized what was happening. His ten- year-old son had earlier asked him to kick around a soccer ball, so he decided to see if he could shift into second gear. Luckily, the boy was still interested, and after about five minutes of kicking the ball back and forth, the play turned into a one-on-one soccer match. They took a tumble and as they lay on the grass both chuckling and panting, Rob looked up at the clouds in the sky. After a few peacefully happy moments, he rolled on his side to look at this son. As he did so, he noticed that the grass was getting pretty long. An idea suddenly came to him that he could help his father-in-law by mowing the big yard.

The next evening when his father-in-law came home from work, he not only found the grass neatly mowed, the edges of the lawn carefully trimmed, but also found a note from Rob thanking him for allowing the family to stay with them. After a hearty handshake and a heartfelt expression of thanks from his father-in-law, Rob thought, "Third gear, and maybe even fourth gear!"

Lesson Two Homework

For maximum benefit do this assignment before going to chapter three.

1. Give an example of recognizing yourself in first gear.

_____

_____

_____

_____

_____

_____

2. Give an example of consciously going from first gear to second gear by doing something which involves both your mind and your body.

_____

_____

_____

_____

_____

_____

3. Give an example of being in third gear by doing something which involves the use of your mind, body, and spirit in helping another person.

_____

_____

_____

_____

_____

_____

4. Explain to another person at least one of the ideas of interest to you from the lesson. Briefly describe your experience.

_____

_____

_____

_____

_____

_____

If interested, please watch the video "High Pressure Thoughts"
by scanning the QR code.

Chapter Three

The Road

Rob was the first to raise his hand when Dr. Vreda asked for people to comment on how their assignments went from last week. Rob shared the experience of playing soccer and mowing the lawn, and for several minutes the class had a lively discussion about his use of the gears. A woman pointed out that when Rob was looking at the clouds, he was probably in neutral for a few moments, and then he "heard the music." Dr. Vreda complimented them on their perceptiveness about the gears and told them that tonight's discussion would further build their understanding.

"Let's jump into tonight's topic, which is entitled 'The Road'. Let me start out with a question. Please raise your hand if you have ever ridden on a highway where along the side of the road, outside the white line, was a series of small bumps built into the asphalt which some people call rumble strips."

Rob, along with all of the other class members, raised his hand. Dr. Vreda continued, "Those bumps are irritating! Why did somebody build something irritating along the edge of the road?" he asked smiling.

A couple of class members responded at the same time, "To wake you up," "To keep you from drifting off."

Dr. Vreda continued playfully, "Well, why is that important?"

Rob said, "If you go too far off the road, you can crash."

"I want to raise your awareness this evening. Each of us has a smooth road on which to travel, flanked on both sides, by a series of rumble strips. The road is what we are going to call 'The Present', or in other words, the immediate here-and-now. If we go too far to the right, the vibration of the rumble strips lets us know we have drifted mentally into the uncertain future. If we happen to drift clear across the road to the left, the uncomfortable vibrations of those rumble strips let us know we have drifted into the rocky past of unpleasant memories. Let me show you this in picture form on this transparency."

Dr. Vreda then placed a transparency entitled "The Road of Life" on the overhead projector.

"As you can see, there are a band of rumble strips several feet wide along both sides of the highway. Outside of that relatively small band of rumble strips, there are progressively larger sets of bumps, until they are about the size of speed bumps, such as those found on a school property. If you have ever hit one of those unaware, you know how jarring they can be! Those larger bumps on the Road of Life are more intense, bothersome emotions, which are there to vigorously warn us

The Road

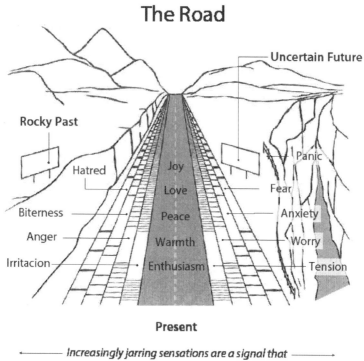

Uncertain Future

Rocky Past

Hatred | Joy
Love | Panic
Biterness | Peace | Fear
Anger | Warmth | Anxiety
Irritacion | Enthusiasm | Worry
Tension

Present

——— Increasingly jarring sensations are a signal that ———
you have strayed from the
highway of reality

if we have strayed from healthy thoughts. If you look here to the left hand side, there is a message which says, 'Notice: Increasingly jarring sensations are a signal that you've strayed from the highway of reality."

At this point, one of the class members raised her hand and asked, "What do you mean by the highway of reality? The past and the present and the future are all part of reality, aren't they?"

"That is a deeply important question," responded Dr. Vreda sincerely. "If we can only answer that one question this evening, our time will be well spent. Let me attempt to answer by sharing a quote. One famous psychologist, Fritz Perls, said, "Unfortunately most people rarely show up for their life while it is being lived."

There was some soft chuckling among the class members, and Dr. Vreda went on, "When I first heard that statement, I also had to laugh because I realized that I had spent many years not 'fully showing up for life.' The principle of 'fully showing up for life' marks the distinctive line between the highway of reality and the less real experience of attempting to live emotionally in a place other than where you are right now. For example, even though our bodies are here at the library in this particular room, a portion, and in some cases a large portion, of our individual minds might be somewhere else. In that regard, you are not fully showing up for the class tonight. This is what happens each time we let our minds wander either to unpleasant memories from our past or to uncertainties about our future.

All of us are at least a little bit out of alignment and need to be aware of where we tend to drift. For example, I tend to be out of alignment to the future, and if not careful, I will begin drifting toward and overly focusing on the future."

Another hand went up and a person asked, "Well isn't it good to focus on the future? I mean, to plan ahead and be prepared is good."

"This is where some subtleties of excellent driving come into play. Let me quote from a fun little book entitled The Precious Present by Spencer Johnson: 'It is wise for me to think about the past and to learn from my past. But it is not wise for me to be in the past. For that is how I lose myself. It is also wise to think about the future and to prepare for my future. But it is not wise for me to be in the future. For that, too, is how I lose myself'(Doubleday, 1992, p. 48-49)."

"The best answer I can give you at this point is that our future planning and goal setting work best in a neutral and pleasant state of mind. This is how we can have inspiration and form a positive vision for reaching goals and solving problems. If we attempt to focus on the future in a first gear mode, we tend to feel anxious--as if we are already living in an unpleasant future, and may, in fact, begin a negative self-fulfilling prophecy process."

"I am not sure if I have fully addressed your question," said Dr. Vreda.

The class member answered, "I'll have to think about this some more. It's a new idea for me."

Another hand was raised and the class member asked, referring to the diagram, "What do you mean by the panic out there by the edge of the cliff?"

Dr. Vreda explained, "Out past the distant edge of the future oriented rumble strips is an intense warning which we call panic attacks. This is when the heart beats so fast that people describe it like a heart attack or feeling that their heart is going to beat out of their chests. Another common panic symptom is the extremely frightening sensation of not being able to get enough air. Some individuals describe this as feeling a heavy weight on their chest. I have never personally experienced one, but from what my clients have told me, few things are more frightening. I like to compare a panic attack to a guardrail along the side of a highway, which we smack up against when we have gone way too far off the road. This is such a frightening experience that many people are willing to seek mental health services and to try different approaches to life in an effort to prevent such an experience from happening again."

"One of the traps of being on the rumble strips is that if you don't know what is happening, the jarring emotions of anxiety and fear can cause us to place even more importance on our thoughts. Also, in those states of mind, our heart begins thumping noticeably, similar to the sound of being on a rumble strip."

At that point Dr. Vreda vigorously patted the left side of his chest with his right hand, creating a rapid thumping sound similar to hitting a rumble strip.

"A lot of people, when they have such a strong physical reaction, believe that what they are thinking about must be of tremendous importance to be accompanied by such a reaction. In such circumstances, if we let our thoughts run rampant, they become even more vivid as if our fears become true, right before our eyes."

"Take a look at the milder, initial future rumble strips of tension and worry. The trouble with these two is that although they are uncomfortable, a person is still able to ride on them without feeling in danger or out of control. As an example of this, I drove for about thirty-five years with one set of tires on the worry rumble strips on the Road of Life. I knew I was a 'worry wart', but felt that was just my lot in life and that there was not much I could do about it. I was amazed when I heard of certain individuals who claim to rarely, if ever, worry and just thought that they must be a fluke. For some reason, I felt that if my life was not full of tension and worry, I was somehow not doing my full share. So I went, day after day, thumping away with worrisome thoughts on my mind. I didn't know, until in mid-life, that there was a smooth road available not too far away from where I had been traveling for so long. In fact, every once in a while, I got onto the road of the present when I was doing something like fishing or playing with my dog. I felt more at peace, but it also felt unfamiliar, and I thought that I was somehow shirking my duty to not feel tense."

"As I have learned to 'drive' better, with my mind more often in the present, a fascinating thing has happened to me. Staying on the road used to be an effort as I learned to compensate for my pattern of drifting to the future. I am now realizing that the present is where my being wants to travel and that it is a lot of work to be off to the future. I like to think of the tension I experienced as though I was sticking my head out of the window of the car while still attempting to drive. If the car is like my body and my head position is like my mind, the further the two start to separate, the tougher it is to maintain control. It was a tremendously freeing experience to realize that much of my feeling of being out of control and anxious was not from my circumstances, but was from the direction I was leaning mentally. I would appreciate some input to see if this is making sense from your experience."

One of the men in the room raised his hand and said, "I remember a few years ago we were on a family vacation in the mountains, and when the pavement ended we had to go about ten miles on a fairly washboard-like road. The road was so bumpy that it almost made me want to turn around, but we continued. A couple of days later on our way back out, I was startled this time by how very smooth the highway was after getting off of the rutted dirt road. It dawned on me that on the way out the washboards in the road hadn't bothered me so much because I had gotten so used to them. Only when I hit the pavement did I realize how bumpy they actually were. I couldn't help but think that my vacation had been like going on the smooth road after the tension and worry from work. I hadn't realized how tense I was until we got out of town and out into the mountains. I vowed I was going to try to take the peace I had felt on our trip with me, but it didn't last very long."

Dr. Vreda responded by saying, "That is a great example! It points out something that is very important in this whole process. The best part about having the flu is the increased gratitude for your health when you start to feel better. In the normal course of life, we experience a wide range of emotions, and even young children can distinguish one emotion from another. For example, everyone can feel the contrast between feeling angry and feeling happy. But, like in your example of the washboard mountain road, you can become accustomed to a particular emotional state of mind and begin accepting that as your only option."

A woman raised her hand and asked, "Is it possible to go back and forth between the future and the past? It seems like I do that a lot."

"Yes, most definitely," Dr. Vreda responded. "In my experience with working with people and also in trying to understand myself, there seem to be two ways to do that. The more common pattern is what I'll call swerving in and out: dwelling on negative things from the past and then projecting them into the future which then brings about even more intense bitterness and resentment about things that happened in the past. This back and forth swerving which increases in intensity, is often part of clinical depression. In fact, I often think of depression as a recipe whose main ingredients are a constant mixing of anger and fear. If you put those two emotions together in a beaker, the mixture is black and murky and stinky!"

A number of the class members chuckled and Dr. Vreda asked, "By the raise of hands, how many of you think that depression stinks!" It appeared that all of the class members raised their hands, some more heartily than others, and Dr. Vreda said, "The reason that it stinks is to encourage us to not like it. Depression is the epitome of not being in the present and not showing up for life. I have personally been there, and my mind was on anything but the present and certainly not on anything hopeful or encouraging."

"But what if your present stinks?" asked a man in the back of the class. Several class members laughed softly, but the deflated and somewhat sharp tone in the man's voice communicated the personal nature of the question.

"Your question, I believe, is an example of the second type of being in both the past and the future at the same time. I'll portray this as the road becoming so narrow that a person can ride with both sets of tires on the rumble trips on the sides of the road. In such situations, it is as if the road does not exist and all there are rumble strips. A man who was painfully agitated most of the time, pointed this out to me very vividly a few years ago. When I shared with him the Road of Life diagram, he said, 'Do you want to know how life feels to me? It's like I'm riding on a bicycle, and the road is just barely wide enough for my bicycle tires and I'm almost always on the rough sides. A lot of the time it feels more like I am on my bicycle, but riding between the rails on a railroad track, constantly being jarred by hitting the railroad ties and simply holding on for dear life.' I have found that when a person described his or her life that way, it has usually been an extended period of time that they have had almost no break from a painful emotional experience. If you ask them, they usually tell you that this notion of finding peace in the present makes no sense to them. It is as if any connection to the present has been pinched off and it doesn't exist. I have found that with some insight and practice, anyone can begin to open up that connection, or in other words find the road."

"We'll finish tonight with a suggestion or two which hopefully will help to put the ideas we've talked about into practical use. Sometime this week you will find yourself feeling the agitating rumble strips. When you do, I encourage you to first of all recognize that you are straying in your thoughts from the present. Secondly, I encourage you to identify the emotion you are experiencing. I find it personally helpful to pause and actually tell myself the emotion I am having. Next, check to see if your thoughts are, in fact, going in the predicted direction based on your emotion. For example, if you are feeling angry, examine your thoughts to see if you are recalling and dwelling on other times of trouble or frustration the person you are angry with has caused you. Once you have identified your emotion and the direction of your thoughts, you are now aware of which side of the road you are. That is a very important step in being aware of yourself, and to then be able to take control of yourself."

Dr. Vreda then asked a question, "If you were literally driving a car and found yourself straying off the road at high speed, what is the first thing you want to do?"

A man next to Rob said, "You first want to take your foot off of the gas and start slowing down. You don't want to make any sudden turns toward the road or you might over-correct."

"That's right," said Dr. Vreda. "You want to begin slowing down, and that's what you want to do when you are on the emotional rumble strips. Allow yourself to stop pursuing the agitating thoughts in your mind by literally slowing down your pace. Stop whatever you might be saying, either out loud or in your thoughts, and take a few deep breaths. This can help.

As you can see, as you focus on your breathing, you are connecting better with your body. Tying this in with last week's lesson, what gear are you shifting into by focusing on your breathing?"

Rob responded by saying, "You are shifting into second gear by involving both your mind and body."

"That's correct," smiled Dr. Vreda. "Do the rest of you see how that is a second gear action?" The class members nodded and Dr. Vreda continued, "After you feel yourself starting to slow down, focusing on the breathing can also help you ease yourself back on the road. You can then help yourself not revert to first gear and to stay in second gear by doing something productive with your body beyond focusing on your breathing. This will further help you to come back to the immediate present, and off of the rumble strips. Here's an assignment sheet where you can record your experience. Please give it a try and we'll talk about it next time. I hope you all have a good week!"

On the way home from the library, Rob was so excited about what he had learned in class that he couldn't wait to get home to tell Linda about it. When Rob arrived at home he saw Linda sitting on the front steps and he began telling her about things like rumble strips and the present.

After he slowed down a little, Linda said in a fairly flat tone, "It sounds like you really enjoyed the class. I'm glad you did." Rob could tell that Linda wasn't having a good evening, and Linda asked if they could go for a walk in the neighborhood and talk privately. Rob wondered what was up and immediately went on a walk with Linda.

They walked for a few tense moments in silence, until Rob said, "I sense that you're upset. Is it something that I did?"

Linda didn't know exactly how to start, began to say something, hesitated, and then said, "Maybe I'm just tired tonight, but I'm really feeling frustrated. I'm worried that we are wearing out our welcome here with my folks, and I'm starting to feel mad about the fact that we ever moved away from our friends and our house and everything. Why couldn't you have just kept your job, even though it wasn't the greatest? Here we sit with basically nothing."

Rob was surprised that he was listening to Linda's frustrations more easily than he usually was able and found himself feeling compassion for her. He said, "I'm sorry that you're feeling so bad. It has been really hard trying to start over like this, and I'm sure it has been especially hard on you. I really feel that it's going to work out." Rob put his arm around Linda's shoulders and they walked in silence for a minute. Linda seemed comforted by Rob not being defensive and listening to her.

She asked him to tell her more about the class. Rob began explaining to her things he had learned in the class, and when they got back to the house he showed her the Road of Life diagram. After Linda looked at the diagram for a few moments she said, "I can see myself all over this picture recently. You seem to be learning a lot from this. Maybe I can go with you next week." Rob said excitedly, "That would be great! Maybe we could both work on this week's assignment to see if it helps."

Lesson Three Homework

For maximum benefit do this assignment before going to chapter four.

1. When feeling agitated, recognize that you are straying off of the present in your thinking and briefly describe the situation.

_____

_____

_____

_____

_____

_____

_____

2. Identify the emotion you are experiencing.

_____

_____

_____

_____

_____

_____

_____

3. Look at the "Road of Life" diagram and see if your thoughts are going in the predicted direction based on your emotion.

_____

_____

_____

_____

_____

_____

4. Slow yourself down by taking a few slow, deep breaths.

5. After finding yourself easing back to the present, do something healthy with your mind and body to allow yourself to be in second gear.

_____

_____

_____

_____

_____

_____

6. Explain at least one idea of interest to you from the lesson with another person. Briefly describe your experience.

_____

_____

_____

_____

_____

_____

_____

If interested, please watch the video "The Road" by scanning the following QR code:

Chapter Four

THE FUELS

After being a little nervous about attending the class as a newcomer, Linda was quickly put at ease by a friendly welcome from Dr. Vreda and also the obvious pleasant atmosphere among the other class members.

The class began with Dr. Vreda inviting someone to share an experience based on last week's lesson and homework assignment. A woman volunteered and said, "I was having a terrible time falling asleep a few nights ago. I tossed and turned for about an hour and could not get my mind to quiet down. I felt so helpless and then remembered the homework assignment and thought I would give it a try. The emotion I identified was worry, and my thoughts were on my teenage son. He has been falling behind in school and as he gets more frustrated, it is harder to talk with him about helping with his homework without him getting really angry. I was focusing on how he may not be able to graduate from high school in a couple of years and then what a difficult time he would have finding a good job."

"It became a little humorous to me as I realized my thoughts were several years into the future and that it did match the 'Road of Life' diagram because of me getting way ahead of myself. I did what you said and tried taking a few slow, deep breaths and to focus on the breathing. That seemed to help a little bit, but the worrisome thoughts kept trying to come back, almost like a dog biting at my heels. I continued to focus on my slower breathing for a couple of minutes, and then decided to get up and find something to do. I was about to do some cleaning in the kitchen when I saw the lunch sack my boy had used the day before. I spent a few minutes making an extra special lunch for him to take to school the next day. As I did so, I thought of how much I love him and want the best for him, and a nice feeling came over me. At least I was able to give my son a nice send off to school, after having a fairly decent sleep and sending him out the door with a little care package."

After the woman was finished with her comments, Dr. Vreda said, "That was an excellent job! Could you see how by working through each point on the assignment she was able to better use her energies and have a more positive experience?" The class members nodded and several of them congratulated her on doing a good job. Dr. Vreda then said, "You guys are doing excellent as a class. I can see that you are good driving students. I hope you are having fun with this and are beginning to experience a little more freedom as you practice using the gears and also reading the road more skillfully. It really is a percentage thing. As you begin to increase the percentage of moments that you actually stay on the road, you can get better at shifting gears when different obstacles or challenges may be in your path. Not all roads are flat, are they? Often, we have significant uphill courses we need to take. This training is not just about looking for the easy path, but it is about trying to live our lives more fully and using energies more wisely."

"Tonight's lesson is entitled 'The Fuels', and by the time the evening is over, you hopefully will better understand the three types of fuels to choose from in getting the best mileage in your life. Each of the lessons builds on the previous ones and hopefully reinforces the things we are learning. Each night I present the ideas in a slightly different manner which helps you to better relate to the concept or skill we are talking about."

"I personally learned this notion of the fuels from a psychologist named George Pransky when attending a seminar taught by him in the beautiful coastal city of La Conner, Washington. The days I was there were very exciting because of the new and intriguing coastal landscape, the smell of the ocean, walking on the pebble beaches, and enjoying the tastes of seafood. Perhaps because I was so much in the present and excited to learn, this material made such a deep impact on me. I hope that I can share some of that with you in tonight's lesson."

At this point, Dr. Vreda drew about a one- foot diameter circle on the upper portion of the chalkboard and said, "The first fuel we are going to talk about this evening is the fuel of inspiration. This fuel is what our beings were meant to be fueled on and is obtained when we are in the present. It is a high performance fuel with excellent mileage and actually helps clean our body, mind and spirit."

Next, Dr. Vreda drew a circle about half the size of the other, joining on the left hand side.

"The second fuel I'll briefly describe, has to do with the fuel of the past, which we will call fossil fuel. What are some examples of fossil fuels?"

A class member responded, "Oil, coal and natural gas."

"That's right," said Dr. Vreda. "And do you know what those fossil fuels are made out of?"

The same class member said, "I guess dead plants and dinosaurs."

"Yes. Ancient decaying matter is what produces these fossil fuels, and we fuel our being with these fuels when we are dwelling on ugly and painful memories from the past. In contrast to physical fossil fuels, which are dead and decaying, we have the ability with mental fossil fuels to bring those old dinosaurs back to life. What you think about grows and not only can bring these dinosaurs back to life, but by regularly thinking about them, they grow from small to huge, and then they seem to follow us wherever we go."

Dr. Vreda then drew a circle opposite fossil fuel, which was also adjoining the larger circle and said, "The last of the three fuels is called the fuel of imagination, and is what we fuel our beings with as we are overly focused on the 'what-ifs' of the future. We have probably all had our imaginations run away with us at times. Just like the fossil fuel dinosaurs grow, the fuel of imagination can cause our fears to quickly grow to what we imagine to be our worst nightmares. The fluid nature of these fuels can be compared to a circus balloon, where the clown can twist different portions of the balloon to make toy animals. It is the same amount of volume in the balloon, but depending on how it is squeezed and tied, the different sections have different sizes."

"We are almost never totally fueled by the fuel of inspiration. Those experiences probably come in times of intense natural highs, what psychologist Abraham Maslow termed 'peak experiences.' More often we have a mixture of the fuels and the percentage of the mixture greatly effects us. Basically, this fuel mixture effects every aspect of our being, such as our posture and our outlook. For example, you can usually tell by someone's facial expression which fuel is dominant in his or her mixture. If people have a snarly look on their faces, you can rest assured that their thoughts are mostly related to the unpleasant past—either things that they were angry with others about or things that they were angry with themselves for doing or not doing. On the other hand, if you could measure the thoughts of a person whose face was tense or fearful looking, those thoughts will be about things that have not yet happened but which they fear will happen."

"If you are tracking me, you are probably beginning to wonder how tonight's discussion is different from last week's about the road and the past, present and the future. Have any of you been asking yourself that?"

Basically everybody in the class nodded and Dr. Vreda said, "This week's discussion is further laying a foundation for better understanding ourselves on an even more sophisticated level, and I hope that that will be apparent as the lesson progresses."

"As a little quiz, I am going to show you several diagrams which represent a particular person's fuel mixture and have you tell me which fuel is dominant and what the person is probably experiencing. Where are this person's thoughts mostly focused?"

"The past," several class members said in unison.

"That's correct and as you can see with the fossil fuel dominant in the person's being, the person looks angry. Okay, let's try another one. Where are this person's thoughts mostly focused?"

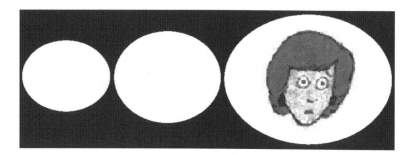

This time, most of the class responded, "The future."

"Very good," said Dr. Vreda. "And as you can see, the fuel of imagination has transformed our person into a being filled with fear. Okay, let's try another one. Where are the thoughts in this person's mind?"

Several class members responded by saying that the person's thoughts were both in the future and the past, with very little in the present.

"Okay, that's right. Can the rest of you also see what they are saying?"

Rob and Linda looked at each other and nodded along with the rest of the class members. Dr. Vreda continued, "This last one reminds me of a Volkswagen Bug sandwiched between two huge semi-trucks on a highway. This is what it feels like when our thoughts are going back and forth between the unpleasant past and the scary future. This results in a feeling of depression. The very small center circle represents us when our present is nearly pinched off. It is important to know that the fuel of inspiration is available to us, but we need to open up the pipeline, which is in the present, to have access to it. I like to think of opening that pipeline as being similar to the expanding of the pupil of the eye or the lens of a camera. It is as if the present is a living thing we can practice with to make more flexible and be able to open more readily."

"I really like the saying, 'The past is history, the future is a mystery, and today is a gift. That's why we call it the present.' All of you have probably heard the suggestion of 'living one day at a time.' If you view the present as being today, your present is defined as twenty- four hours long. The present can also refer to the much shorter time frame of 'the moment.' At times when life becomes very rough it is helpful to reduce life down to the smallest possible unit of living, which is the present moment. When we reduce life down that small it can seem much more manageable. This is similar to the old saying, 'By the yard it is hard, but by the inch it is a cinch'."

"We'll finish tonight with an exercise that can be helpful to anyone but is most helpful for people whose present has become too restricted or nearly pinched off. I call this exercise 'Come To Your Senses'." Dr. Vreda distributed a handout and began explaining the homework assignment.

"Who would like to name our five physical senses?"

Rob raised his hand and said, "Hearing, seeing, smelling, tasting, and touching."

"That's correct," said Dr. Vreda. "Do any of you not have the use of any of those senses?"

A woman raised her hand and said, "I still have them all, but my hearing is getting worse."

"Would you agree with me," asked Dr. Vreda, "that we don't appreciate our senses enough? These are precious gifts that can greatly enrich our lives but which we tend to use way too little. Using these gifts of our senses is a beautiful way of opening 'the present.' As children, these senses were new and exciting and we couldn't wait to do things, such as taste a Popsicle, look at a cow, touch a kitten, smell a flower, or hear a particular song. As we grow older, we often become more absorbed with thinking rather than sensing, and miss much of what is actually going on around us. Our senses are an anchor to the immediate present and as we begin to use our senses more intensely, we begin to be on the road of life more consistently. We then experience more peace, enjoyment, and enthusiasm."

A class member raised her hand and said, "With the senses being part of our body, this reminds me of what we talked about before--about second gear being using your mind and your body. Is this kind of what you are saying?"

"Exactly! I'm really glad that you brought that up," Dr. Vreda said excitedly. "We're starting to see how some of what we have been talking about is related. Our body is always in the present. It can't go anywhere else. Our mind is the slippery part, which can get off track. Really focusing on our senses brings both our mind and body together in the present to better enjoy life. Let me give you a practical example."

Dr. Vreda opened a folder and pulled out a wrapper from a fast food sandwich. "Several years ago, I was on a trip alone and stopped to get a quick hamburger. I was pressed for time and sat down to eat my hamburger while thinking about what I needed to do later that day. A couple of minutes later, I looked down at the table and the burger wrapper was laying flat. I glanced around to see where my burger might be, and then cupped my hand near my mouth and exhaled and smelled onions on my breath. What had happened to the burger?" Dr. Vreda asked with a smile.

"You ate it," said several class members.

"That's right," said Dr. Vreda. "Why didn't I know I had eaten it?"

The class members were getting into the story and without raising their hands, made comments such as, "You had too much on your mind," and "You were eating it without thinking about it."

"How could I have spent those few minutes focusing on that hamburger? Do you think that I could have used all of my five senses while eating it?" Dr. Vreda sought comments from the class such as how he could feel the texture of the bun, taste the pickle, hold the burger close and smell the meat, hear the crunching of the lettuce, and see the various colors, including the redness of the ketchup.

Dr. Vreda then continued, "I would like to suggest to you that I would have been a better person five minutes later if I had allowed myself to use all of my five senses while enjoying that burger. Instead, I got lunch but actually missed the burger. The reason I am emphasizing this is because the more we practice using our five senses, the more we are on the road of the present and the more we are showing up for life. As you use and appreciate your five senses more, you begin receiving a bonus--a sixth sense. You have all heard the term, 'sixth sense.' What does this refer to?"

Rob raised his hand and said, "Intuition."Another class member said, "An unconscious hunch."

Dr. Vreda responded, "Yes, those are common descriptions of the sixth sense. Other terms that are used to describe it are inspiration and insight. I like to think of the sixth sense as coming from the inside out, whereas the other five senses bring information from the outside in. It is as if when we bring fresh sensory information from the outside into our being, it is like pouring fresh water into a stagnant pond. As we experience those five senses more often, our connection to the present expands--almost as if a road opens up in front of us. This is also like cleaning our wind shield and then being able to see much better. New possibilities come into our awareness through our sixth sense. You can see I am getting a little carried away here. I apologize for having the class run over, but this has been a vital thing for my own life, and I wanted to share it with you."

"What about the assignment? How do we complete this form?" asked a class member.

"I'm sorry. I almost forgot that. You make an experiment of consciously using each of your five senses, five times a day, for at least five days this next week. So, it's 5 x 5 = 25, and you record very briefly on this form what you were focusing on," Dr. Vreda explained. "For example, under smelling you could write 'lilac.' To write that down, it would mean that you have not only smelled a lilac quickly in passing, but you took an extra moment to really drink in the smell. I want you to also record the words with your non-dominant hand. This causes you to focus just a little bit longer on what you experienced. It also will look as if a young child has written it. That has a purpose also-to remind us that as children we really knew how to use our senses. On the other form, you will see a space to record any sixth sense impressions which may come to your mind. These will be pleasant, hopeful and fresh ideas to help improve some area of your life. Go ahead and record those with your dominant hand to try to capture them fluidly."

As class was wrapping up, a woman said, "For the last two lessons I have gotten the impression that you view remembering the past or thinking about the future as bad or unhealthy things. I know for a fact, that remembering things or thinking about things in the future can be extremely helpful. How does that fit in with what we have been talking about?"

The class members were very curious to hear how Dr. Vreda would respond. He said, "I really appreciate the question. Do any of the rest of you have the same question?

Most of the class members said yes.

"That question is a sign of your readiness for some even more advanced driving training. Our time is up for tonight, but we'll handle that first thing next week. In addition to the

'Come to Your Senses' assignment, please give some thought to the healthy aspects of thinking about the past and the future and we will hopefully put that into context for you. Have a great week!"

On the way home from the library, Linda knew exactly what she wanted to do to complete her homework assignment. After the children were in bed, she allowed herself to really focus on the taste of the chocolate bar she had in her dresser drawer. Before she took the second bite, she held the chocolate to her nose to take a couple of lingering smells of the thick and sweet aroma. She listened attentively to the splashing of the water as the tub filled and was intrigued at the formation of the bubbles from the bath oils she gently poured where the bath water was churning. And oh, the sense of the touch she focused on as her body submerged under the almost too warm water.

"I like this kind of homework," thought Linda.

Lesson Four Homework

For maximum benefit do this assignment before going to chapter five.

Each of our five senses are marvelous gifts which we often do not enjoy enough. The purpose of this exercise is to practice appreciating our senses more.

1. Use each of your 5 senses at least five times per day.

2. Immediately after using one of your senses, record the name of what you sensed (i.e., "yellow flower" under the sense of smell).

3. Record the item with your non-dominant hand (i.e., with your left hand if you are right-handed) on the pages provided.

4. There are pages following for you to do this exercise on five separate days.

5. See the bonus page to record any personal insights you have from your sixth sense along the way.

Day 1 Date:

Seeing	Hearing	Touching	Smelling	Tasting

Day 2 Date: _____

Seeing	Hearing	Touching	Smelling	Tasting

Day 3 Date: _____

Seeing	Hearing	Touching	Smelling	Tasting

Day 4 Date:

Seeing	Hearing	Touching	Smelling	Tasting

Day 5 Date: _____

Seeing	Hearing	Touching	Smelling	Tasting

Bonus!

If you appreciate your five senses on a regular basis, you get a bonus-a sixth sense! Whereas your five senses bring fresh information from the outside in, your sixth sense brings fresh ideas from the inside out. Record below (with your dominant hand) any fresh and inspiring insight you receive.

_____

_____

_____

_____

_____

_____

_____

If interested, please watch the video "Come to Your Senses" by scanning the QR code.

Chapter Five

ON A SPIRITUAL PLANE

At the beginning of the next class, Linda and a couple of other class members shared their experiences of "coming to their senses." There were a few chuckles as people showed the actual homework, that in fact did look like little children had written it.

Dr. Vreda then said, "I'm glad that you had fun with that assignment, and I hope it becomes part of your regular self-care, as you remember that our senses are a beautiful way of bringing ourselves back to the immediate present. Let's shift now to attempting to answer the question about how what we've learned so far fits with the fact that there are also good things about remembering our past and thinking about our future. What are some of your ideas concerning this? Let's start this discussion by first talking about what some good things are about having a memory."

One of the class members raised her hand and said, "One thing I can think of is to not repeat things that gave us trouble or mistakes we have made that caused us grief. I guess what I am trying to say is,so that we can learn from our experiences."

"Okay, very good: to learn from our bad experiences so that we can hopefully not repeat them. You can also see how that pertains to not just our own life experiences, but learning from other people and even from history." Then Dr. Vreda said with a smile, "It's been said that 'smart people learn from experience, and wise people learn from other people's experience.' Are there any other reasons you can think of what a memory is good for?"

A man raised his hand and said, "Sure, what about all the good times we want to remember--all the fun experiences and the goals we have achieved? Those things are really an important part of life."

Dr. Vreda responded, "You're right! It's really hard to picture what life would be like without a memory of the good times. There is a lot we could talk about here, but let's turn now to the question of why we have an imagination. What is our imagination good for?"

Rob raised his hand and said, "Our imagination helps us to be creative and come up with new ideas to improve our lives. I guess it also is part of what helps people invent new things."

"Good," said Dr. Vreda. "Some especially creative people are able to picture things that nobody else has thought of. Another use of our imagination is to picture what we want to be like as we try to improve ourselves. These brief examples of the good aspects of our imagination and memory are in contrast to the things we have talked about in previous lessons: How our memories and imaginations can be used to dwell on unpleasant things which are dark, heavy, and weigh us down. When we focus our imagination and memory on pleasant and growth-enhancing things we feel more uplifted and enlightened. That leads us into tonight's topic entitled 'On a Spiritual Plane'. So far, we have used the comparison of driving a land vehicle, but for tonight's topic, we need to switch the comparison to a flying vehicle, because we are going to be talking about ups and downs."

"Let's talk for a few minutes about some of the reasons we have ups and downs in life. By this, I mean our mood changes from feeling uplifted and happy to feeling sad and downhearted. What have been some of your experiences or experiences of others that lead to even small changes in our up and down moods?"

"Tiredness! I can easily get discouraged and overwhelmed when I get too tired," said a woman near the front of the class.

"Very good," said Dr. Vreda. "Let's make a list of these things on the board."

Other comments class members made were feeling physically sick, hormone changes, such as a woman's monthly cycle, going too long without eating or eating really heavy foods, and times of increased stress and pressured time deadlines.

"Let's look at some common features about each of these conditions. Have you noticed that when you are down, even little problems look big?" There were many nods among the class members.

"Just like if we were in a small airplane and saw a little red barn on the ground, if we swooped down close to it the barn

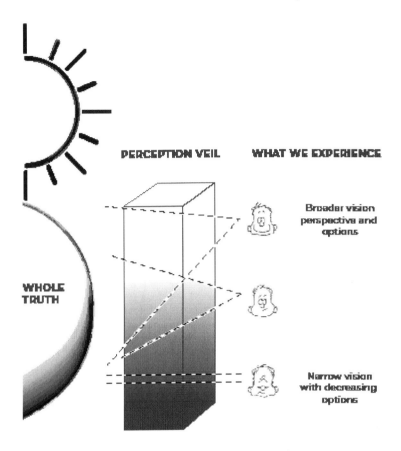

PERCEPTION VEIL   WHAT WE EXPERIENCE

Broader vision
perspective and
options

WHOLE
TRUTH

Narrow vision
with decreasing
options

would grow in size before our eyes. The barn hasn't really changed in physical size. What has happened?"

"You got closer to it," said a number of class members in unison.

"That's exactly right, and this is an important point to recognize concerning our moods. Everything looks bigger when you are feeling low, and the lower you are, the bigger they seem. And, on the other hand, if your altitude and level of 'up-ness' increases, things are more in perspective. Let me show you a diagram which has really been of help to me in dealing with the ups and downs of life."

"I want to share with you now a concept that has been one of the most helpful things that I have ever learned. When your moods are up and you are experiencing a pleasant and peaceful feeling, you are actually more wise and intelligent than when you feel upset and under a lot of pressure. As shown in the diagram, as our mood goes down, our perspective and vision narrows. I like to think of the narrowing vision as giving increasingly tighter sensations or feedback that our vision is in fact becoming more narrow. I want to emphasize that the smaller the vision, the 'dimmer' our intellect. To put it bluntly, the lower our moods, the dumber we become. The trouble is we get too dumb to know that we are dumb!"

Most of the class members chuckled and nodded in agreement. "Let me give you just a quick example. I'm very much a morning person and everything seems more clear and doable in the mornings. I remember in high school when I would get tired at night, I would be getting upset about how hard my math homework was. My mother would often say to me, 'Just get some rest and it will all look better in the morning.' This often frustrated me even more,because how would the same math problems be any different in the morning? But my mother was right! Somehow the same problems seemed smaller and easier after a good rest."

"You may be asking yourself what this has to do with remembering or imagining. I need to put this in a context to be able to better explain good and bad memories and good and bad imaginings. To do this, we are going to picture ourselves in a small airplane at different elevations and either tilting or not. We are going to compare the altitude of the plane to our moods and compare the tilt, either to the right or to the left, as to our time orientation. Tilting to the left will be looking to the past or remembering, and tilting to the right will be looking to the future or imagining. When you are at a high altitude in a good mood and look toward the past, we are going to call that reminiscing. When you are reminiscing, you have the full picture of your view--both the beautiful memories and the lower painful memories--but the painful memories are far away and in perspective. At that higher level we find it naturally easier to be forgiving. We can be more forgiving of ourselves for past mistakes and also more forgiving of things that others have done, which have caused us trouble in the past."

"When at a high mood altitude, and you lean more toward focusing on the future, we are going to call that dreaming. Dreaming implies having the full view of the future with its exciting possibilities, along with potential fears, which are much smaller in perspective. At that high level, we find it easy to trust, because we are operating out of a position of inner security. If you were physically in an airplane and leaned the plane to one side or the other, and did this for a long time, what would happen to the direction you were going?"

A man raised his hand and said, "You would begin turning and banking toward that side. If you kept doing it long enough you would be going in a big circle."

"That's right," said Dr. Vreda. "Can all of you picture what he is talking about?" The classmembers nodded.

"The point I am trying to make here is if you were going in a certain direction that was in front of you, it is okay to look briefly to the left (reminiscing) and look briefly to the right (dreaming), but not to do that too long to the neglect of your present life situation and your desired course. This goes back to what we talked about before of life in its fullest form happening right now in the present."

"Okay, we have been talking about being at a high altitude. Now let's switch to when you are flying at a low altitude--in other words, experiencing life through a low mood. As you become more familiar with your internal instrumentation you can better recognize when you are low. When you are low and know that you are low, you are much better able to deal with life than when you are low and don't realize that you are low. That can really be dangerous! I am sure all of us can recall things we have done or said when we were in a low mood that we have regretted later. Sometimes we just can't immediately get out of a low mood but need to know how to cope with it when we are down there. When you are flying low, that's not the time to be looking anywhere but straight ahead. It's dangerous at those times to be leaning one way or the other. Those low times are when the mind tends to be easily distracted and wanders to looking at the negative past or future. Because when we are down, there is much more darkness in our awareness than light. There is, however, in the very tight, dark state of mind, a tiny light at the end of the tunnel that we need to focus on rather than on the surrounding darkness."

A man raised his hand and said without waiting, "Hey, you're losing me! Can you put this in more practical terms, please?"

Dr. Vreda directed the question to the class to see if anyone was grasping what he was saying.

A woman raised her hand and said, "I think I am following you. When you are low, it's very easy to get caught up in focusing on the bad, from either your past or your future, which then only makes you go even lower and more likely to crash. At those times, you need to focus just on right now and take things one step at a time."

Dr. Vreda turned to the man who had the questions and asked, "Does that make more sense?"

The man responded, "A little, but I still needsome practical examples."

Dr. Vreda again asked for class input and another man said, "I think I can give an example here. After I went through a divorce, about three years ago, I was really depressed and was just beating myself up all the time about my past mistakes. I was not only down on myself about my relationships but also about some bad decisions I had made in jobs. It seemed like I was doing a life review of all the low spots. I also was really afraid I would never have a good relationship with my kids or anybody else. I could hardly sleep at all and finally, to cope, to be able to keep going to work, I started walking my dog every morning to get some exercise and try to clear my head. I gradually was able to recognize more when I was beating myself up and tried to be gentler on myself just to survive day-by- day. As I started healing a little bit more, I was surprised to realize

I was mentally complimenting myself about past accomplishments and other things that showed I was a good person. It had been so long since I had such thoughts that they seemed kind of strange to me.

I guess from what you are telling us tonight, my plane started to go a little higher and then I was able to lean more toward the past without only being able to see the bad things. From your comparison, my altitude was high enough that I could see both the bad and the good things, but the bad were down lower, so they weren't quite as big as they had seemed before when I was really low."

Dr. Vreda again sought feedback from the man who had asked the question and this time the man said, "That really helps. I can relate to that type of thing in my own life."

"Are there any other questions at this time?" asked Dr. Vreda. There was a pause and no one responded so Dr. Vreda said, "We've talked about a lot of different concepts tonight. Let's have a brief review and then I have a question for you. I am going to put some drawings on the overhead projector that show the cartoon character at various altitudes and whether flying level, leaning toward the past, or leaning toward the future. The first drawing shows the person at a high altitude. First of all, is his mood up or down?"

Several people answered simultaneously, "Up!"

"That's right," said Dr. Vreda. Notice how the airplane is tilted toward the past. What do we call the experience we have of remembering the past when in a good mood?"

A woman at the side of the class raised her hand and said, "Reminiscing."

"That's right," said Dr. Vreda. "Is that clear to everyone?"

People in the class were nodding their heads and Rob understood that concept better now.

"Okay, the next drawing shows a man at a high altitude and in a good mood and tilting toward the future. What do we call that experience?"

Rob raised his hand and said, "Dreaming." "That's right!" said Dr. Vreda. "Okay, now let's look at some drawings of a person flying in a low mood. This guy is low and tilting toward the future. What is he experiencing?"

"Panic," "Fear," said several class members simultaneously.

"When you are low and you know you are low, is that the time to be focusing your thoughts on the future?"

Several of the class members were shakingtheir headsno.

"Let's look at the drawing of the person flying in a low mood and looking toward the past. What does it appear that this person is experiencing?"

"Anger," "He's mad," "Full of rage," said several of the class members.

"From what we have learned this evening, what do we need to do when we recognize we are in such a state of mind?"

A man raised his hand and said, "We need to fight against the tendency to dwell on dark things from the past or the future and instead focus straight ahead in doing things right now, just a step at a time."

"That statement you just made has been one of the most helpful things I have learned in terms of coping with life's challenges. I hope that these examples can help you understand these ideas and navigate better during the down times. I've been using phrases like 'going in the right direction.' What do you think I mean by the right direction for your life?"

Nobody responded and after a few moments Dr. Vreda said, "It's a tough question, isn't it? The idea of a right direction for our lives implies that there is a plan or purpose for each of us. I would like to share with you my personal view that this really is the case for each of us and that God knows what that purpose is. It is very important for us to have quiet time on a regular basis to be able to ponder, in a neutral state of mind, the direction our life is going, and if what we are doing on a day-to-day basis is going to help us end up where we need to be. Often, where we think we need to be may be different from the real plan for our lives. I once saw on a billboard a statement that made this point. It read, 'If God is your copilot--change seats'."

Several class members chuckled softly and Dr. Vreda asked, "How would you say that in your own words?"

A woman said, "Let God be the one directing your life. He knows what is best for you."

"Thank you for your good comments and participation this evening," said Dr. Vreda. "We have just one more lesson to go, which will continue to build on the knowledge and experiences we have been having together. We'll see you next time."

On the way home from the library, Rob and Linda didn't talk much. They were in somewhat sober and contemplative states of mind as they reflected on the things that were discussed in the class. Rob spoke up and softly said, "I really need some direction in my life."

After a few moments Linda responded, "I really feel that same way too."

Lesson Five Homework

For maximum benefit do this assignment before going to chapter six.

1. Make a list of situations or factors which contribute to you being more vulnerable and in a low mood.

_____

_____

_____

_____

_____

_____

2. Catch yourself when in a lower mood and recognize the pressure and tightness as indicators of your reduced perspective and limited vision. Briefly record your experience.

_____

_____

_____

_____

_____

3. Recall a time in life when a situation seemed overwhelming and later the same situation seemed more manageable when your mood was higher. Briefly record your experience.

_____

_____

_____

_____

_____

_____

4. Make time in a peaceful setting to ponder the purpose and direction of your life. Record your thoughts.

_____

_____

_____

_____

_____

If interested, please watch the video "How Much of the Truth We Perceive" by scanning the QR code.

Chapter Six

EMOTIONS MAP

"Well, here we are for the last class already," Dr. Vreda said with a smile. "You have been super participants and overall a great class. I would love to have you drop me a line in the future, if you would like."

"Let's start out tonight with quoting the very first line from the book by M. Scott Peck, entitled 'The Road Less Traveled'. Do any of you know what the first sentence is? It's a very shortsentence."

Nobody answered and Rob also didn't know. He had read the book years ago but didn't know what the first sentence was.

Dr. Vreda said, "The first sentence of that book is, 'Life is difficult.' At first glance, it's kind of a negative statement, isn't it?" Several class members laughed softly.

"Luckily, that's not the end of the story. As we look a little deeper, we realize that difficult is not necessarily bad. We have all done things that were difficult that we can see were very growth enhancing for us. Whether it's mastering a particular skill, enduring a time of hardship, or mourning for someone else's hardships, those experiences help to shape our character. Life is interesting because of the variety of experiences we have. I've heard it said, 'If music only had high notes, it would simply be noise.' It is the combination of high notes and low notes that makes both music and life interesting."

"We usually understand things best by experiencing their opposite. For example, you can never really appreciate health as much as when you are recovering from being sick. Tonight, in our last lesson we are going to be looking at what I call the 'Emotions Map'. It is a combination of opposites which builds upon some of the things we have talked about in previous lessons. I would like to suggest to you that even though life is difficult, it can be experienced with joy. Life being difficult and being experienced with joy are not two incompatible ideas. Though life is difficult, it does not mean that it is not right or that it is somehow a big disappointment. I have a belief that one of the goals of life is to learn how to experience it with joy, even though it is difficult."

"This emotions map that we will talk about tonight is maybe better defined as an emotions window. In this window, about a foot above our heads, is a circle of absolute clarity. When we are looking out through that spot, everything is clear, in perspective, and all makes sense. The feeling we have when looking out of that portion of window is what we call joy - a deep combination of peace and happiness. Away from that clear spot, the window is at least somewhat distorted, and what we see becomes more distorted the further down and away from that spot. The distance away from that spot, and also the direction away from the spot, have predictable, emotional sensations, which actually indicate to us where we are in relation to the clear area of joy."

A woman in the class raised her hand and asked the question, "If you're talking about looking through this clear part of the window, why did you say that it is above our head? It seems like it would be down here where we could see out of it."

"Thank you for asking that question," responded Dr. Vreda. "I meant to clarify that and forgot. The reason that it is a little above us is that it requires our spirit to be uplifted for us to see out of it. A normal, everyday view, at eye level is already starting to get a little bit distorted. We are going to say that joy is actually a combination of faith, hope, and love. Each of these are high-quality states of being and can be developed and refined by each of us." On the chalkboard above the circle with the word "Joy" in it, Dr. Vreda drew an intersecting circle with the word "Hope" and asked, "What is the opposite of hope?"

A man answered, "I would say despair."

"That word really captures it, doesn't it?" said Dr. Vreda, and wrote "Despair" straight down below the "Joy" circle. "Despair is at the extreme end of the continuum of sadness, then depression, and then hopelessness or despair. Notice how each of these feelings have an increased amount of pain, and that increasing painfulness is a signal that a person is getting further away from the clear perceptions of joy, and are experiencing increasingly distorted perceptions and thoughts."

On the right side of the "Joy" circle, Dr. Vreda drew an intersecting circle with the word "Faith" and asked, "What is the opposite of faith?"

A woman in the front row raised her hand and said, "I would say doubt."

"I would agree with you," said Dr. Vreda, "But to make it fit this model, could we use the word fear?"

"I guess that would make sense," the woman said smiling.

"Increasing levels of fear are experienced the further away we are from faith, such as what we have talked about in the past, including worry, fear, and panic. Again, the pain increases and the level of distortion becomes more pronounced the further away we are."

Dr. Vreda then drew an intersecting circle on the left side of the window of "Joy" with the word "Love" and asked, "What is the opposite of love?"

"Hatred," said several class members in unison.

"If you were to look into the mind of a person filled with hatred, and we've all felt versions of that in the past, you could see much darkness and distortion. The pain associated with resentments, bitterness, and hatred feels terrible, as we all know. They are letting us know that we are missing life as it was meant to be lived."

Dr. Vreda then put a transparency on the overhead projector and showed the emotions map with each of its parts.

"As I have been using this map to guide me for several years, it has helped me to spend less time in more negative and painful states of mind. It has been helpful for me to have a whole

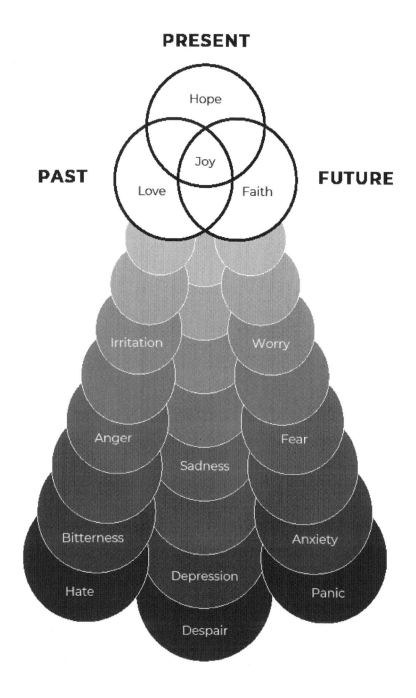

context to plug my experiences into. I would like to compare the use of this map to a game I used to like to play as a child. Have any of you ever played the game that I call the Warmer-warmer Cooler-cooler game? This is where you hide something in the room and give directions to another person by saying, 'You're getting warmer' or 'You're getting cooler'." Basically everyone in the class nodded or said that they had played the game.

Dr. Vreda continued, "It's a fun game. How does the cooler signal help you to find what you are looking for?"

Linda answered, "It lets you know that you are going in the wrong direction--that you need to try a different way."

Dr. Vreda responded, "That's right. How does the warmer signal help you to find what you are looking for?"

Several class members said, "That you are going in the right direction and getting closer."

"Exactly," said Dr. Vreda. "I have come to believe that this must be God's favorite game. I believe that he is playing it with us all the time, because the thing that he wants us to find is joy. This map can be a guide to us when we are feeling cooler in our emotions; the thoughts and direction we are headed are cooler in our hearts. Then we can use some of the ideas and techniques from these lessons, or other means, to turn around and head in the warmer- warmer direction. It works for me, and I encourage you to give it a try to see if it seems to be of help to you."

"Before we end class tonight, let's do a little reviewing. Lesson 1 was about a century of driving. Do any of you happen to recall anything out of that particular lesson that has been of help to you?"

A man raised his hand and said, "I think that was the lesson where I learned that the use of my mind was way too dominant over the use of my body. It dawned on me that as an adult, I have not only neglected my body, but also felt okay about it because most of my productive activities had to do with using my mind. I guess I was kind of swept along with our modern culture."

"Very good observations," said Dr. Vreda. "Just that realization that you have had can be very helpful. I am glad that was useful to you."

"Okay, the second lesson was on the gears. Did any of you find something helpful there that you would like to share with us?"

Rob responded to this one and said, "Just having it explained in terms of gears was very helpful for me to know what was happening when I was feeling better or worse mentally. I think that I have actually been able to get out of first gear more often and also accept neutral as a legitimate place to be at times."

"Let's move on then to Lesson 3, which was about understanding the road."

A woman spoke up and said, "Oh that was my favorite lesson! I've got the picture of the road on my refrigerator and have made copies for a number of my friends. I hope that was okay?"

The class members and Dr. Vreda laughed, and he said, "I won't tell anybody if you don't. What did you like about the road?"

The woman continued, "I don't know. It just made a lot of sense. I guess the idea that has been most meaningful to me is that the mental rumble strips are now a warning to me. But before the class, they were just the beginning of me feeling like I had to think more about what I was dwelling on."

"Wow, that is wonderful," said Dr. Vreda. "I wish everybody knew that. Feel free to keep passing those pictures around."

"Lesson 4 was about the fuels. Any comments or things that you found helpful in that lesson?" said Dr. Vreda.

Linda was the first to respond and said, "That was my first time to class and it made a big impact on me." Rob playfully joined in and said, "Yeah, she's been taking a bubble bath about everynight!"

The class members and Dr. Vreda laughed and Linda continued, "It's hard to say what it's done for me, but I somehow just feel a little safer and more peaceful-- more like I felt as a child when there weren't so many worries."

Dr. Vreda commented on how that was what the teachings of these lessons had done for him, too, in a way that was hard to describe. "We have seen how the lessons have built on each other, and last week we tried to put the ideas from the lessons into use, in not only driving, but also piloting to higher levels. Would anyone like to mention anything that might have been helpful out of that lesson?" asked Dr.Vreda.

A man in the class said, "The part about letting God give me direction in my life has been really challenging to me. I guess I really hope that can happen, but don't have too much confidence in it yet."

Dr. Vreda appeared serious and said, "I really appreciate your honesty. I imagine each of you came to this class with the hope of getting some help for your lives. Most people don't have extra time to do something good for themselves unless they really need it."

Dr. Vreda's comments reminded Rob that although he had enjoyed the lessons and felt noticeably better over the last several weeks, he still had not found a job and was feeling without direction in a number of areas of his life. That realization made Dr. Vreda's next comments even more meaningful to him.

"I want to give each of you a guarantee tonight. From my own experience, if you will keep driving, practice staying in the higher gears more often, staying on the road more often, using a better fuel mixture, and keeping at a higher altitude, answers and direction will come. I have found that God whispers, and the more often we have a mind that is quiet and clear, we are able to better hear the whisperings. You can better recognize those whisperings when you realize they are accompanied by feelings of peace and joy. That's where the warmer-warmer comes in."

"We've had some fun in these classes and I hope that it has been a good use of your time. There is a lot more that we could talk about, but I would like to end by encouraging each of us to make it a lifetime endeavor and adventure to develop more faith, hope, and love. As those become more of a regular part of our lifestyle, we will experience joy more often. That joy will be a deep source of feedback to us that we are heading in the right direction, even though times may be hard. I sincerely hope that the things we have talked about in this set of lessons will help you to find joy a little more often. Thanks again for being such a great group."

For more chapter six resources, please watch the video "The Emotions Map" by scanning the QR code.

About the
Author

Ryan J. Hulbert

Ryan J Hulbert, Ph.D., graduated from Brigham Young University, and received his doctorate in clinical psychology from the University of Nebraska-Lincoln, with sub-specialties in alcoholism treatment and rural community mental health. In 1986, he completed a research fellowship at the Catholic University of Louvain, Belgium where his fascination with the role of time perspective in human functioning began.

Dr. Hulbert served as a staff psychologist and Director of Research at the Cherokee Mental Health Institute in Cherokee, Iowa from 1988 and 1993. He was the Chief Psychologist of BPA Behavioral Health for eight years, and was the Clinical Services Administrator for the Idaho Department of Juvenile Corrections from 2001-2009. In 2010, he assisted in the initial program development for the Management & Training Corporation's Correctional Alternative Placement Program (CAPP), in Idaho. Beginning in 2015 he has taught psychology courses as an adjunct faculty member at Boise State University.

He is the author of several articles in professional journals, has presented numerous workshops, and is the author of the books *The Sun Is Always Shining, Drivers' Ed for the Brain, Growth Rings, Eternity-Time-Eternity, Which Came First, The Soul or the Ego?, No Longer Settling for Half of the Rainbow,* and *Divine Potential: A quest for truth.* He is also the inventor of The Support Team Game, and the developer of Roots and Branches: A multigenerational holistic training program for everyday hero individuals, families, and communities.

He is the founder of EPIC Psychological Services, with "EPIC" being an acronym for "Empowering People in Communities." His professional mission is to "brighten the light, warm the heart, and enhance the health of his clients, colleagues, and community." He views his strengths as compassion, creativity, and enthusiasm, in working with others to enhance health and reduce human suffering through increasingly effective, accessible, and cost-effective methods.

He and his wife, Theresa, have five sons, two daughters, five daughters-in-law, two sons-in-law, and a growing number of grandchildren. They live in the country near Parma, Idaho. Dr. Hulbert very much enjoys spending time with his family, fishing, helping others, and doing family history research.

Aknowledgments

I would like to express my deep appreciation for a number of people who have been highly instrumental in bringing this book to completion. My wife, Theresa, has been my biggest support and typed the original manuscript. My research mentor, Willy Lens, at the Catholic University of Louvain, Belgium first introduced me to the intriguing and powerful role of time perspective in human functioning. William Pettit MD, and George Pransky, Ph.D. provided much inspiration in viewing people as being naturally healthy and at times needing guidance to begin to realize their natural strength. Travis Frederickson, founder of Creating Change, provided much encouragement, including printing an initial version of the book in 2007. Rochelle Fowler prepared the manuscript for printing, and Dr. Marwan Sweedan gave helpful insights and enthusiastically pushed for its publication. Marijke Grant did the final formatting of the book.

It has been a fun experience attempting to convey simple yet powerful concepts through the teaching style of Dr. Vreda.

For more information visit us at
DRIVERSEDFORTHEBRAIN.COM

Made in the USA
Middletown, DE
24 February 2023

25584097R00064